I belong in every space I walk into

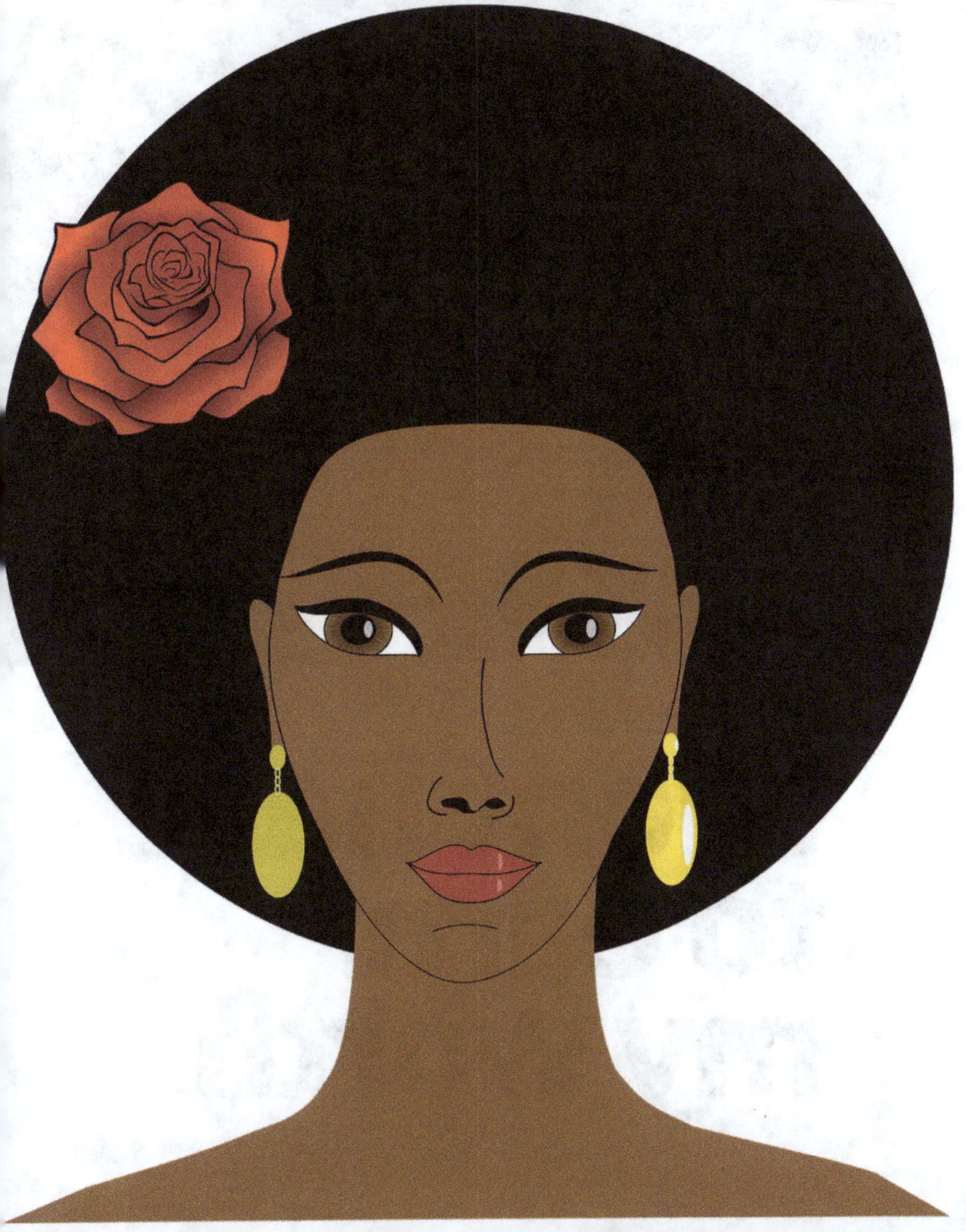

Being me is how I win

I am unconditionally worthy

I allow myself to feel so I can heal

I release what doesn't reciprocate my energy

I prioritize my peace

I am becoming a better version of myself each day

I am energetically aligned to all I desire

My Black is radiantly beautiful

I am comfortable saying "no"

Money loves me, Money always returns to me

I will not settle for less than the best in myself and others

I am grateful for every experience

I am worthy to be loved and to love unconditionally

Everything I want wants me too

I will not let what others say or do get me off track

I am focused on being a better me

I love myself unconditionally at all times

My ideas are valuable

I deserve a seat at the table

I deserve a soft life

I deserve a life of luxury

My hair texture is unique and beautiful

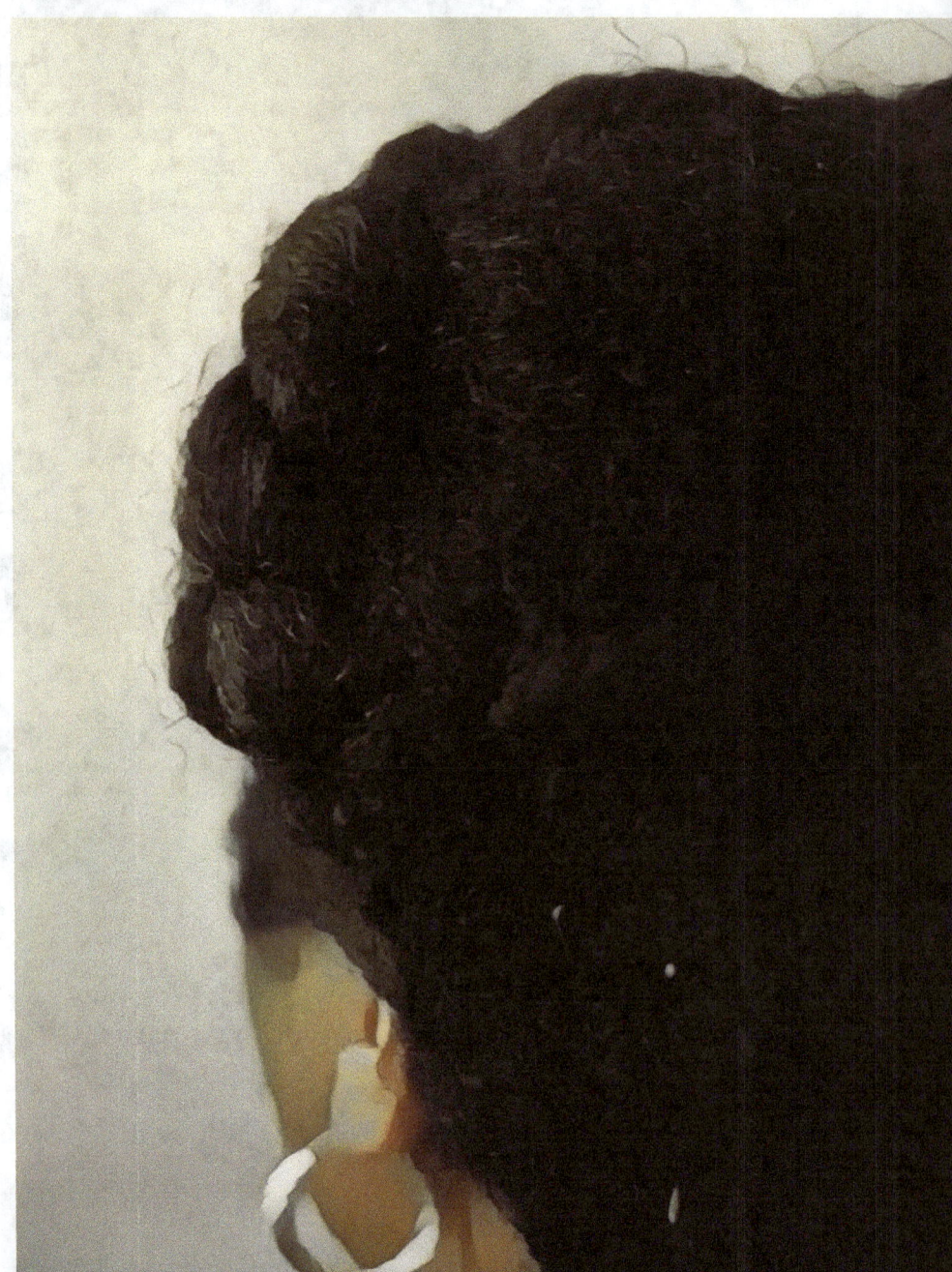

I am financially abundant

Today and everyday, I choose joy

I surround myself with peace and pleasant emotions

I will thrive and not just survive

I am an asset to my community

I give myself permission to do what is right for me

Abundance is my birthright

I love the skin I'm in

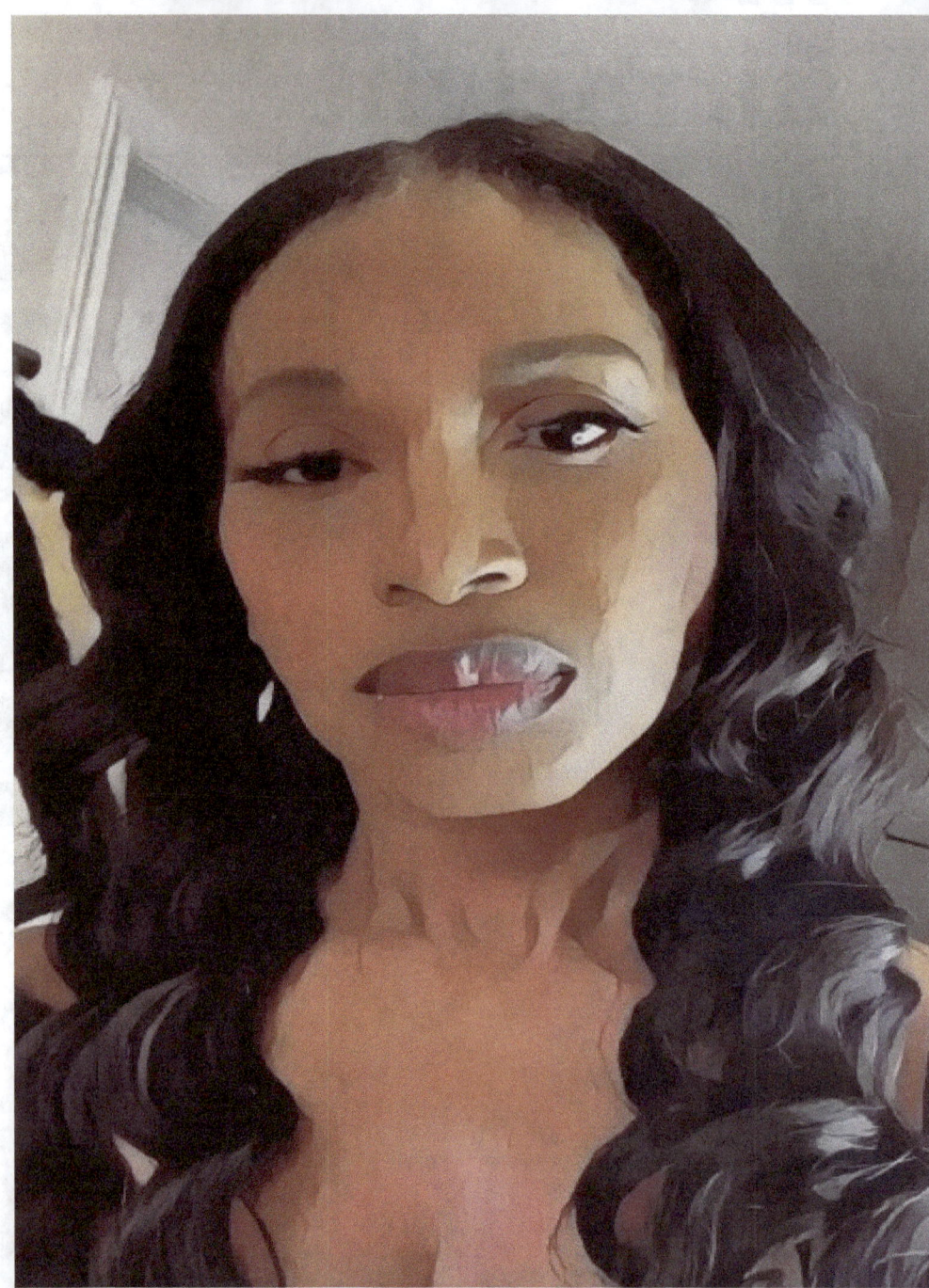

I am proud of my cultural heritage

I will always hold my head high

I am in charge of how i feel and i choose happiness

I am a work in progress and my progress never ends

The insignificant actions of others do not have to impact my life significantly

I matter, my beliefs matter, my voice matters

Its ok to smile when I'm happy, cry when I'm sad, show gratitude when I'm thankful

I am healing all internal wounds

Happiness, peace, laughter, wealth surrounds me because I'm worthy

I attract success

I am intelligent and successful

All my goals are

manifesting

I release all forms of self-doubt

Fear will not control me

I attract people who will help me to reach my goals

I know I'm on the right path

www.ingramcontent.com/pod-product-compliance
Lightning Source LLC
Chambersburg PA
CBHW070339120526
44590CB00017B/2951